Where Is Massachusetts?

Where Is Massachusetts?

by Laurie Calkhoven

illustrated by Ted Hammond

Penguin Workshop

For Colleen, who is living a glorious life
in Massachusetts—LC

PENGUIN WORKSHOP
An imprint of Penguin Random House LLC
1745 Broadway, New York, NY 10019
penguinrandomhouse.com

Designed and Produced by Dinardo Design, LLC.

Library of Congress Cataloging-in-Publication Data is available.

First published in the United States of America by Penguin Workshop, 2026

Manufactured in the United States of America
CJKW

ISBN 9798217243068 (paperback)
10 9 8 7 6 5 4 3 2 1

ISBN 9798217243075 (library binding)
10 9 8 7 6 5 4 3 2 1

The authorized representative in the EU for product safety and compliance is Penguin Random House Ireland, Morrison Chambers, 32 Nassau Street, Dublin D02 YH68, Ireland, https://eu-contact.penguin.ie.

Contents

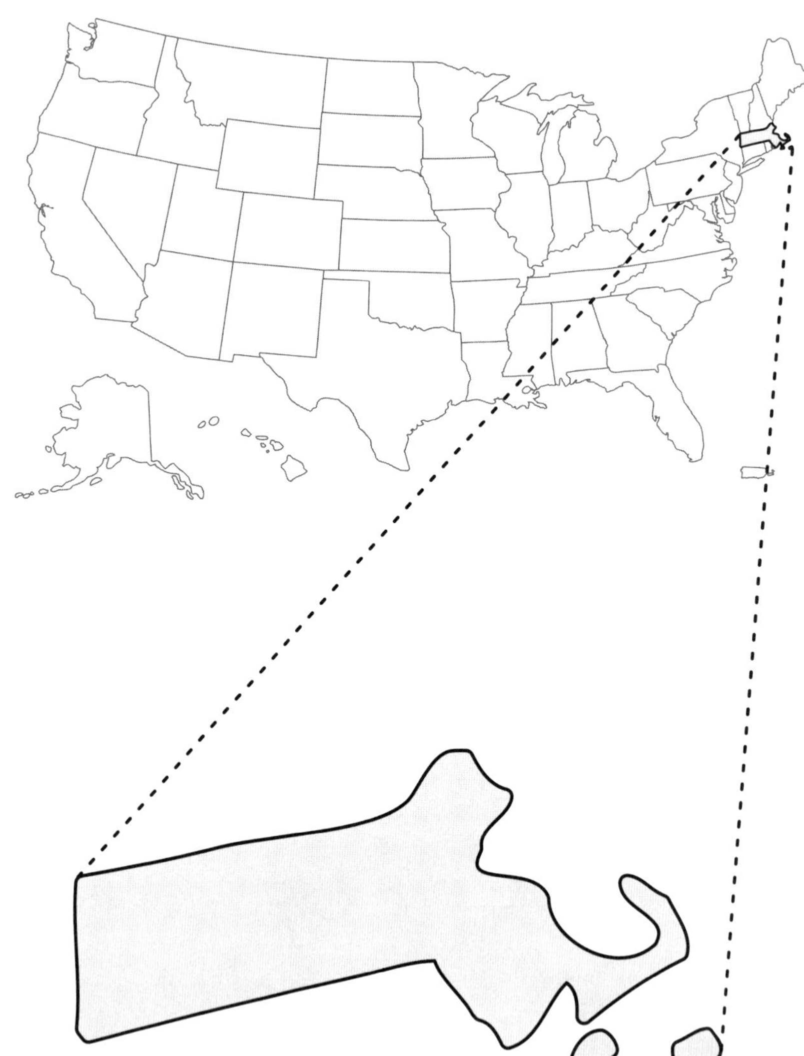

Where Is Massachusetts?

Massachusetts is the seventh-smallest US state in terms of area. It's also a northeastern state, far from the geographical center of the country. Yet it has been at the heart of US history from the beginning.

The land was named after the Massachusett Tribe, an Indigenous people who have lived there for thousands of years. Another Indigenous group, the Wampanoag (say: waam-puh-nog), helped the first English settlers survive. In time, Massachusetts became one of the thirteen English colonies that fought for their independence and declared themselves the United States of America.

From Plymouth Rock to Paul Revere, Massachusetts is often the first place that comes to mind when thinking about the story of the

United States of America. This small state has continued to be a part of American culture, from the creation of the chocolate chip cookie to the invention of basketball! Massachusetts may be where the fight for American independence began, but it's also a place where people have made decisions and discoveries that have continued to shape the nation.

CHAPTER 1
The Land and Its People

Massachusetts is one of six New England states and has a total area of 10,554 square miles. It shares borders with Vermont and New Hampshire to the north and Rhode Island and Connecticut to the south. New York lies on its western border, and the eastern boundary is defined by the Atlantic Ocean.

The coastline was formed about eighteen thousand years ago. Glaciers, or large sheets of ice that move slowly over land, scraped and shaped the earth. This created the many bays (bodies of ocean water partially surrounded by land) that form the Massachusetts coast today. Massachusetts is known as the Bay State. Famous Cape Cod is a peninsula (piece of land surrounded

by water on three sides) that looks like a giant fishhook. It's named for the many codfish caught in its waters. The coast has pristine beaches and bogs (areas of soft, wet land) that are ideal for growing cranberries, one of Massachusetts's most important crops. There are also freshwater and saltwater marshes which serve as nesting grounds for many types of fish, birds, amphibians, and reptiles, such as the eastern box turtle.

Two farmers in a cranberry bog

In the center of the state, plains and rolling hills are crisscrossed with rivers and streams. Apples, vegetables, and Christmas trees are some of the crops grown there. The western part of the state is home to the Connecticut River Valley and the Berkshire Hills, which include Mount Greylock, the state's highest point at 3,491 feet. The Berkshires are part of the Appalachian Mountains, one of the oldest mountain ranges on Earth.

Forests cover more than 60 percent of Massachusetts, making it a perfect place to see the leaves change color every fall. Eastern white pine, red maple, eastern hemlock, and northern red oak trees fill these forests, which are home to animals such as deer, beavers, coyotes, skunks, red foxes, and chipmunks. Playful river otters pop their heads through holes in the ice in the winter. They also love sliding down snowy hills! Black bears had almost disappeared from the state by the 1940s, but today, the bear population is around 4,500. Reforesting (planting new trees where the land had been cleared) is the main reason.

More than three hundred types of birds can be found in Massachusetts. Some are permanent residents, such as wild turkeys. Others are passing through on their annual migrations. Sandpipers, herons, and egrets live near the coast, where the waters are filled with marine mammals, such as whales, and many kinds of fish.

The earliest humans living in what we now call Massachusetts were Indigenous peoples who arrived in the area more than ten thousand years ago. Many nations, including the Massachusett, Wampanoag, Nauset (say: naw-sett), Pennacook,

North Atlantic right whale

and Pocomtuc (say: POH-cum-tuck), farmed, fished, and hunted there. They created villages and roads and often traded with each other. Their languages all belonged to the Algonquian (say: al-GON-kwee-uhn) language family, and they are sometimes grouped together as the Algonquian people. The Algonquian people didn't have written languages. Grandparents and parents shared stories out loud with children about their history and culture.

Their homes, called wetu (say: WEE-too) or wigwams, were dome-shaped wooden frames covered in mats woven from cattails or tree bark. A hole at the top of the wetu let out smoke from cooking fires. When the villages moved to new locations, they left the frames behind and took the mats with them. That way, they could rebuild their homes when they traveled from coastal fields, where they grew corn, beans, and squash, to inland hunting grounds as the weather grew colder. Some groups lived in longhouses that could shelter as many as four families. All of them built canoes to fish off the coast and in rivers.

Many historians believe that Viking explorer Leif (say: leaf) Erikson, from what is today Iceland, was the first European to reach North America around 1000 CE. Other Europeans from England, France, and Spain began fishing in the waters near Massachusetts in the 1500s. They traded with Wampanoag people and sometimes kidnapped and enslaved them.

Wampanoag means "People of the First Light." There were nearly forty thousand people in the sixty-seven villages that made up the Wampanoag Nation in the late 1500s. But Europeans brought diseases with them that Wampanoag people had never been exposed to, including smallpox. It is estimated that between 50 and 90 percent of Wampanoag people died from diseases such as smallpox in the early 1600s.

CHAPTER 2
The Pursuit of Freedom

On September 16, 1620, a ship called the *Mayflower* set sail from England for the colony of Virginia. There were 102 passengers on board. Some were Pilgrims who had left England in search of a land where they could practice their religion freely. They were punished at home because they did things differently from the official Church of England. They had permission from the King of England to settle in the Virginia Colony, which had been established in 1607.

Storms had pushed the ship north, and the Pilgrims sailed into Cape Cod Bay in November of 1620. When the ship tried to travel south, it ran into rough, shallow waters. The Pilgrims decided to find a place to settle near Cape Cod instead of the Virginia Colony.

The Pilgrims didn't have permission to form a colony there. Some men on the ship didn't want to help build the new settlement because it wasn't in Virginia. Before they set out to investigate the land, the men on the ship reached an agreement. This agreement, called the Mayflower Compact, said that the group would elect a government and follow its laws. The men on the ship signed the compact. It was the first document to establish that men in the colonies could choose their own government.

The Pilgrims decided to settle in Plymouth, where they found an abandoned Wampanoag village with plenty of water and nearby farm fields. The Wampanoag people had been devastated by European diseases before the Pilgrims arrived, which made it possible for them to take over.

The Pilgrims didn't know how to survive in this new land, and they arrived too late in the year to plant crops or gardens. Many died in the long, cold winter. A Wampanoag leader named Massasoit (say: MA-suh-soyt), also called Ousamequin (say: O-suh-meh-quin), approached the Pilgrims and offered his help. Another man named Squanto came with him. Squanto, who was also known as Tisquantum (say: TIS-quan-tum), had been enslaved and brought to Europe, where he learned English. He returned home in 1619 to discover that most of his people had died.

Together, Squanto and Massasoit taught the Pilgrims how to survive by planting corn, squash, and beans, and how to hunt and fish. Squanto even tried to convince the Pilgrims to bathe. The Europeans believed that washing their whole bodies was unhealthy. They just washed their hands and faces, and sometimes only once a week!

With the help of Squanto and Massasoit, the colony survived. The Wampanoag people hoped they'd gained an ally after so much death

from disease. The next fall, the Pilgrims and the Wampanoags celebrated the harvest with a feast now known as the First Thanksgiving.

The story of the First Thanksgiving has often been told to make the relationship between the Pilgrims and Indigenous people seem simple, which was not the case. It's likely that this First Thanksgiving was less of a celebration than many claim. A peaceful relationship didn't last. This was part of a violent takeover of Indigenous land

and resources by European colonists.

The Pilgrims began to thrive, and that attracted more colonists. In 1630, another group, called the Puritans, arrived and founded the Massachusetts Bay Colony. Over the next ten years, more than two hundred ships sailed from England carrying twenty thousand people. They made the settlement of Boston their capital. Located on a harbor, this village quickly grew into a small city.

The Puritans also established the very first college in North America, Harvard College, in 1636, in Cambridge (then called Newetowne). Although the college mostly educated white men and was founded to educate ministers, Caleb Cheeshahteaumuck (say: CHE-shah-tee-ah-muck) of the Wampanoag was the first Indigenous person to graduate in 1665.

The Puritans, like the Pilgrims, wanted freedom to worship in their own way. They had strict rules, including that everyone had to go to church. They forced anyone who did not practice Christianity their way to leave the colony—including Indigenous people. The Puritans wanted to force the local Wampanoag people to live, speak, and worship like they did. They stole Wampanoag land and destroyed Indigenous villages. Their settlements grew. In 1691, England united the Plymouth Colony, the Massachusetts Bay Colony, and Maine (a territory north of

Massachusetts) to form one big Massachusetts Bay Colony. The islands of Nantucket and Martha's Vineyard (near Cape Cod) were also merged with the colony.

Many Puritans living in the colony believed the devil could hurt people and witches helped him. In the town of Salem, in 1692, two young girls got strange illnesses. Soon, more girls and women began acting strangely. They claimed that witches had made them ill. They accused some of their neighbors of working with the devil. More than two hundred men and women were accused of being witches. Twenty innocent people were found guilty and killed before the odd behavior and accusations in Salem died down.

Conflict between the Puritan and Indigenous communities continued. The Puritans took more and more land. As a result, some Indigenous groups sided with the French during the French and Indian War (1754 to 1763). This war was fought between the French and the English for control of North America. By the end, England controlled most of eastern North America. Fighting was expensive, and England taxed the colonies to cover its costs.

By 1765, there were more than 220,000 people living in Massachusetts. Boston was an important port that traded goods from England, Europe, and other American colonies. It was in Boston that the colonists first began to protest against England. Even though colonists were forced to pay taxes, they had no say in the government. The colonists' slogan was No Taxation Without Representation. They began to boycott (stop buying) English goods. When that didn't work, there were more protests.

Some colonial leaders thought a place in the English government wasn't the solution. They supported freedom from England. These patriots, who called themselves the Sons of Liberty, included Samuel Adams, John Adams, John Hancock, and Boston silversmith Paul Revere, who had a successful business making things such as tea sets and bowls out of silver.

Violence erupted between the colonists and English soldiers on March 5, 1770. Colonists surrounded an English soldier and threw insults and objects at him. He called for reinforcements, and a small group of soldiers faced off against the colonists. One of the soldiers fired a shot, leading to more gunfire. Five colonists were killed, including a sailor of African and Indigenous ancestry named Crispus Attucks. The Sons of Liberty called the event the Boston Massacre, and Attucks and the others who died were seen as heroes.

When colonists refused to accept shipments of tea from England and threw them into the harbor, the English punished Boston by closing the port and filling the town with soldiers. The people of Massachusetts became even more angry.

The Boston Tea Party

The colonists were angry about the English tax on tea. The English were also trying to control where the colonists could buy tea from. On Sunday, November 28, 1773, a ship called the *Dartmouth* arrived in Boston Harbor carrying 114 chests of tea. Two more ships, the *Eleanor* and the *Beaver*, followed. The Sons of Liberty refused to allow the tea to be unloaded from the ships because of their boycott. The governor of Massachusetts, who was loyal to the King, refused to allow the ships to return to England with their tea. It was a standoff.

The colonists decided to show England how serious they were. On the night of December 16, about sixty men poorly disguised as Indigenous people boarded the ships. Some of them were probably Sons of Liberty, but we're still not sure. They ordered the captains and crew to go below

decks and then tossed 342 chests of tea into Boston Harbor. Today, that tea would cost around $1.7 million!

The Sons of Liberty celebrated the raid as a victory, but the English government shut down Boston Harbor and filled Boston's streets with soldiers. This set the stage for the American Revolution.

English officers decided to capture the leaders of the Sons of Liberty and destroy the colony's weapons. They were being stored outside of Boston in Concord. The colonists heard about the plan, and they were ready. As the English soldiers slipped out of Boston on the night of April 18, 1775, Paul Revere rode ahead to warn the Sons of Liberty that the English were coming. The soldiers, called redcoats because of the color of their uniforms, and the colonial militia faced off. (Militias were part-time armies that were expected to help the colony when they were needed.) No one knows who fired first, but shots rang out on the Lexington Green the next day. More men and militias gathered in Concord, where battle broke out again. It was the beginning of the American Revolution.

The redcoats retreated to Boston, and the new Continental Army, including about 150 men of Indigenous or African ancestry, formed a ring around the city. The Battle of Bunker Hill followed on June 17. The English won the battle, but they lost twice as many soldiers as the Continental Army, who'd proved themselves to be a dedicated fighting force. After that, the war moved south and continued for eight long years. Finally, the colonies won their independence from England on September 3, 1783.

The new country held the Constitutional Convention, a gathering of representatives from each state to agree on rules of government for the United States of America. The Massachusetts Constitution, written primarily by John Adams, was a framework for the US Constitution, which was signed on September 17, 1787. Massachusetts helped establish the United States as a young country and would be an important part of its future.

CHAPTER 3
Growth, Development, and Industry

After the revolution, Massachusetts continued to grow. The state officially abolished (outlawed) slavery in 1783, although there were already many free Black people there. Many Black people settled in Boston neighborhoods such as Beacon Hill and the North End, as well as on the island of Nantucket.

Nantucket was also known as a center of shipbuilding and whaling. Whale oil, especially sperm whale oil, was a valuable resource. It produced an odorless flame and could be used for safe indoor lighting. Homes, factories, streetlamps, and even lighthouses were illuminated by whale oil. But it was New Bedford that became the home of the most whaling ships in Massachusetts. Herman Melville, who spent eighteen months as a crewman on whaling ships, was inspired to write the novel *Moby Dick*. It was published in 1851.

Melville wasn't the only writer working in Massachusetts. Many American authors lived there while creating their most famous works, including poet Henry Wadsworth Longfellow and essayist Ralph Waldo Emerson. Emerson's friend Henry David Thoreau wrote a book, *Walden*, about building a cabin next to Walden

Pond and appreciating nature. It was published three years after *Moby Dick*. These works, among others, established Massachusetts as a center of American literature, a legacy shared by other writers who lived and worked there in the 1800s, such as Frederick Douglass, Emily Dickinson, Louisa May Alcott, and Nathaniel Hawthorne.

Even as Melville was writing, the whaling industry was slowing down. Overfishing and the discovery of other types of oil led to less whaling. Massachusetts was already looking ahead to the Industrial Revolution.

The Industrial Revolution happened when people started using new materials and machines to make things instead of making them by hand. A lot of people left the countryside to work in new factories in cities. Throughout Massachusetts, businessmen had been opening factories. One man, Francis Cabot Lowell, invented a system to make fabric quickly and cheaply. He hired young, unmarried women and girls from farms and small villages to work in his mills. They stayed in boarding houses and often worked long hours for little pay, but the system made lots of money for Lowell. Other factories opened all over the state to produce textiles (fabrics), shoes, and other goods. There were so many factory jobs that they attracted immigrants from all over the world, including Ireland, Portugal, Poland, and Greece. Even children worked in the factories!

Most factories used raw materials that were shipped from the southern states—materials that came from the work of enslaved people. While factories continued to make money, tension grew between those who believed slavery should continue and those who believed it should be abolished. This tension led to the American Civil War in 1861. The war was fought between the Northern states (the Union) that wanted slavery to end and the Southern states (the Confederacy) that wanted slavery to continue. Massachusetts fought on the side of the Union. One of the first units of Black soldiers in the country was formed in Boston. Men came from all over the city, state, country, and even other nations to volunteer for the 54th Massachusetts Infantry Regiment. They fought in several important battles, including an assault on Fort Wagner in South Carolina. The battle was a defeat for the Union, but the 54th's bravery inspired more than 180,000 more Black soldiers to enlist. They were vital to the Union's

victory in the Civil War, which ended when the Confederates surrendered on April 9, 1865.

Following the Civil War, there was a struggle to establish rights for Black people, who were finally free. Organizations and political groups grew. In 1894, Josephine St. Pierre Ruffin and Florida Ruffin Ridley of Boston started *The Woman's Era*. This was the first national newspaper made by African American women for African American women.

The country turned its attention to other

firsts after the long war years. In 1876, Boston became the site of the very first telephone call in history. Inventor Alexander Graham Bell phoned his assistant in the next room and said, "Mr. Watson, come here. I want to see you."

Another new idea was the sport of basketball. It was invented in 1891 by James Naismith, a physical education teacher at Springfield College. Soon, basketball spread across the country. The world's first annual marathon race was held in Boston in 1897. The Boston Marathon is still run today!

The Boston Red Sox (originally called the Boston Americans) were founded in 1901 and won the first World Series in 1903. They began playing at Fenway Park in 1912, and they still play there. In 1920, one of the team's stars, Babe Ruth, was traded to the New York Yankees. That led to one of the greatest rivalries in baseball. Some people think it cursed the Red Sox and kept them from winning another World Series for decades.

In 1924, attention was on another sport when the Boston Bruins were established. This National Hockey League team would win the Stanley Cup six times over the next century.

Many Boston sports fans were immigrants. Massachusetts was home to people from Ireland and Italy, among many other countries. By the early 1900s, Boston's North End was largely an Italian neighborhood. It was also a busy area that goods were shipped in and out of. When the United States joined World War I in 1917, materials were stored in the North End to help the war effort.

The Great Molasses Flood

In 1919, a huge storage tank in Boston's North End sat full of molasses. (Molasses, a sweet syrup made from sugar, was used to make alcohol as well as weapons during World War I.) Many people who lived in the area believed the metal tank wasn't secure. Molasses seeped through the seams. Children brought buckets to collect it. The tank often made rumbling noises. The company that owned the storage tank did nothing to fix it.

On January 15, the tank burst. More than two million gallons of molasses rushed down the streets of the North End—about 110 swimming pools worth! The wave of sticky molasses crushed buildings and moved a firehouse off its foundation. People and horses couldn't get out of the way. The molasses wave was as tall as forty feet, as wide as 160 feet, and it flowed at thirty-five miles per hour!

Firefighters and police officers from all over the city raced to help. Sailors from ships in Boston Harbor came ashore to aid in the rescue. Twenty-one people were killed, and more than 150 were injured. It took weeks to clean up the fourteen thousand tons of spilled molasses.

The next decade brought the Great Depression. From 1929 to 1939, the US economy was severely weakened. Many people lost their jobs and struggled to earn enough money to keep food on their tables. World War II began in 1939, and the United States joined the fight in 1941. Massachusetts became a hive of activity. The US Navy needed shipyards to build and repair warships. Factories opened to construct planes and weapons. As they had in World War I, many people from Massachusetts volunteered to serve in the military and to work for the war effort.

Even stars from Massachusetts's sports teams did their part. Ted Williams electrified the Boston Red Sox when he won baseball's Triple Crown (best batting average, most home runs, and most runs batted in during a single season) in 1942 before enlisting in the navy. World War II ended in 1945, and Williams returned to Boston. He went on to a whopping career total of 521 home runs.

In 1946, the state that invented the sport got a professional basketball team—the Boston Celtics. The Celtics became one of the most successful teams in the National Basketball Association with legendary players such as Bill Russell. Russell even coached the team while he played. In the thirteen seasons Russell played for the Celtics (1956 to 1969), they were champions eleven times!

The 1950s and 1960s also brought a new generation of a political family. John F. Kennedy (JFK) had been a World War II navy hero. There were popular Boston politicians on both sides of his family, and many of his family members were successful Irish immigrants. Kennedy served in the House of Representatives from 1947 to 1953 and in the Senate from 1953 to 1960, when he was elected the thirty-fifth president of the United States. He was just forty-three years old when he took office. He and his glamorous wife, Jacqueline, and their two children were popular with the American people. Kennedy was assassinated in Dallas, Texas, in 1963.

The 1960s were also defined politically by the civil rights movement. This was a time when Black Americans fought for equal rights and enacted change. At the time, Massachusetts was a state that was largely segregated. Different races and ethnic groups lived in separate communities and went to separate schools. For Black people in Massachusetts, that often meant schools that weren't as good as those in white neighborhoods. In 1965, civil rights activist Dr. Martin Luther King Jr. led a march to protest segregation in Boston. More than twenty thousand people walked from Roxbury to Boston Common, singing freedom songs.

Music often brought people together. In the 1960s, local musicians made their mark on

WE
For
CIVIL RIGHTS FOR ALL!
EQUAL RIGHTS!
EQUALITY!

American culture, and jazz greats from around the world came to perform in Boston. The 1970s brought rock, with bands such as Aerosmith, the Cars, and the Pixies forming in Boston. In the 1980s, the Boston Symphony Orchestra turned one hundred years old!

Music wasn't the only art that was popular in Boston. At the Isabella Stewart Gardner Museum in 1990, two men dressed as police officers claimed to be investigating a disturbance. The men tied up the museum's security guards and removed thirteen priceless pieces of art. The thieves left behind five empty frames after cutting the paintings out. Empty frames still hang in the museum.

Around the same time, Boston became the site of the biggest and most expensive highway project in US history, known as the Big Dig. An underground expressway made up of tunnels beneath the city and Boston Harbor was built from 1991 to 2006. The project created more than three hundred acres of parks and green spaces in the city, but people still joke about how long the Big Dig took and how expensive it was.

CHAPTER 4
Today's Massachusetts

Today, more than seven million people call the state home. Visiting Massachusetts can feel like stepping back in time. The Freedom Trail in Boston is a path that takes visitors through historic sites in the city. Many of the sites played a role in the American Revolution, including Paul Revere's home in the North End. Visitors to Salem can go on haunted tours and look for witches. With the beautiful beaches of Cape Cod, Nantucket, and Martha's Vineyard, and the forests and lakes of the Berkshires in the western part of the state, tourism is one of the state's biggest industries.

Sports fans can see the Boston Fleet of the Professional Women's Hockey League and, starting in 2026, a National Women's Soccer

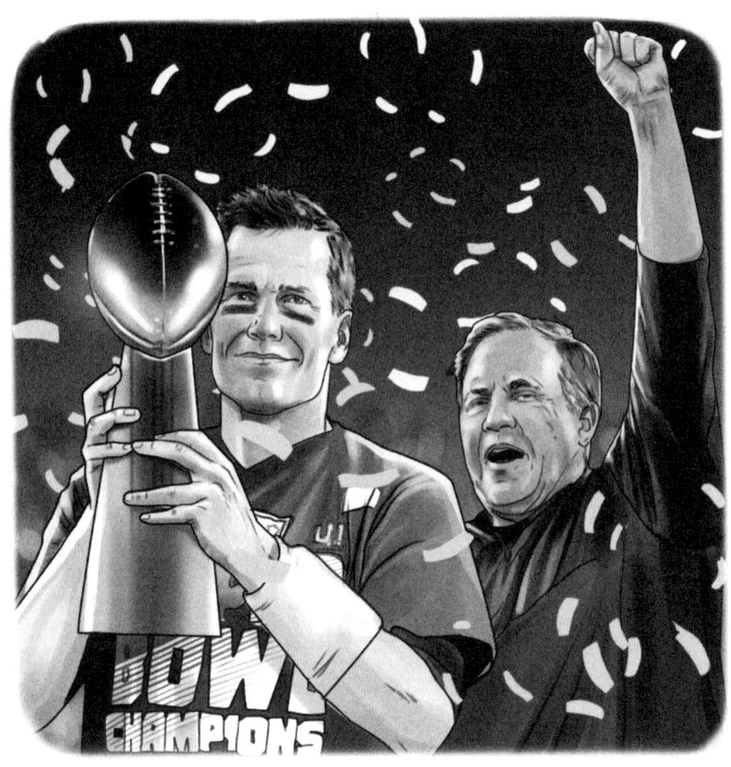

League team. The New England Patriots of the National Football League were founded in 1959. They've won six Super Bowl titles, all led by quarterback Tom Brady. And in 2004, the Red Sox finally broke their "curse" by winning their first World Series since 1918. Players became such big heroes that some, like David "Big Papi"

Ortiz, had streets named after them!

David Ortiz is Dominican American. Massachusetts is home to over one million immigrants, many of whom are from the Dominican Republic, Brazil, China, India, and Haiti, as well as many other nations.

Many people make their homes in Massachusetts's second-largest city, Worcester (say: WUH-ster), known for its eight colleges and universities. The Pioneer Valley in western Massachusetts is also home to many colleges, such as Amherst and Springfield. In fact, Massachusetts's schools are often ranked the best in the country. The Woods Hole Oceanographic Institution on Cape Cod is a world leader in ocean research and exploration. Massachusetts is also the home of the country's first public school and public library.

One of the state's most famous schools, Harvard University, is the place where Facebook was invented by four students in 2004. Today, the company Meta, which includes Facebook, is worth over one trillion dollars!

Don't forget the food. Puritans loved the beans they found in North America. Baked beans were a dish they could cook on Saturdays and eat on Sundays, when they were meant to rest. The dish helped give Boston its nickname, Beantown. The first recipe for New England clam chowder was published in the *Boston Evening Post* in 1751. It continues to be a popular dish all over the state. Order a bowl along with the official state dessert, Boston cream pie. The dessert is believed to have been invented by a chef at a Boston hotel.

Boston Children's Hospital is the top pediatric (children's) hospital in the world. People travel to the state from all over for medical care. Massachusetts was also the first state to allow same-sex marriage in 2004 and to give nearly all state residents access to health care in 2006.

The Indigenous people of Massachusetts continue to be a vital cultural force. In 1987, the federal government formally acknowledged the Wampanoag Tribe of Gayhead as a nation. In 2021, the Department of the Interior confirmed that a reservation on Cape Cod rightfully belonged to the Mashpee Wampanoag Tribe. Members of the Nipmuc Nation continue to live in central Massachusetts. Members of the Massachusett Tribe live in the Blue Hills area of

eastern Massachusetts. They pass many traditions on to new generations in the same way their ancestors did—through storytelling.

The story of Massachusetts includes the Sons of Liberty, Indigenous people, swimming and whale watching in the waters where people fished for codfish, art museums, and watching the leaves change color in the Berkshires. It's important to the history of the United States, as well as to its future.

Massachusetts at a Glance

Statehood: 1788

Nickname: The Bay State

Abbreviation: MA

State Motto: By the sword we seek peace, but peace only under liberty

State Tree: American elm

State Marine Mammal: Right whale

Capital: Boston

Size: 10,554 square miles

Population: Over 7 million

Famous People from Massachusetts: W. E. B. Du Bois (civil rights leader), Clara Barton, (founder of the American Red Cross), Aly Raisman (Olympic gymnast), John Cena (actor, professional wrestler)

State flag

State bird
Black-capped chickadee

State flower
Mayflower

FUN FACT:

In the 1930s, the owner of the Toll House Inn in Whitman, Ruth Wakefield, chopped up a chocolate bar and added the pieces to her cookie dough. America's love for the chocolate chip cookie was born!

Timeline of Massachusetts

8000 BCE	Indigenous peoples make the area home
1000 CE	Leif Erikson sails to the shores of North America
1620	Pilgrims from England arrive in Plymouth aboard the *Mayflower*
1773	Colonists dump 342 chests of tea into Boston Harbor
1775	The Battles of Lexington and Concord mark the beginning of the American Revolution
1788	Massachusetts becomes the sixth state
1814	Francis Cabot Lowell opens his first textile factory
1876	Alexander Graham Bell makes the first telephone call
1919	The Great Molasses Flood rushes through the streets of Boston
1961	John F. Kennedy takes office as the thirty-fifth president of the United States
1990	Thirteen works of art are stolen from Boston's Isabella Stewart Gardner Museum
2004	Massachusetts becomes the first state to legalize same-sex marriage
2018	The Boston Red Sox defeat the Los Angeles Dodgers to win the World Series
2019	The New England Patriots win their sixth Super Bowl

Timeline of the World

1760	George III becomes King of England
1844	Samuel Morse sends the world's first message via telegraph; it says, "What hath God wrought?"
1867	President Andrew Johnson reaches an agreement to buy Alaska from Russia
1869	The Transcontinental Railroad is completed, connecting the Eastern and Western United States
1914	The Panama Canal opens
1920	The Nineteenth Amendment to the US Constitution is officially adopted, giving women the right to vote
1931	The Empire State Building, then the tallest building in the world, is completed in New York City
1969	Apollo 11 lands on the moon carrying Neil Armstrong and Buzz Aldrin
2001	Terrorists attack the United States in a series of four plane crashes
2004	A massive earthquake in the Indian Ocean triggers a tsunami wave that hits the coasts of several countries of South and Southeast Asia
2014	Malala Yousafzai wins the Nobel Peace Prize for her efforts to make sure all girls have a right to education
2022	Russia launches a military invasion of Ukraine

Bibliography

***Books for young readers**

*Crane, Cody. ***My United States: Massachusetts.*** A True Book. New York: Scholastic Inc., 2018.

*Cunningham, Kevin. ***The Massachusetts Colony.*** A True Book. New York: Scholastic Inc., 2012.

*Holub, Joan. ***What Were the Salem Witch Trials?*** New York: Grosset & Dunlap, 2015.

*Krull, Kathleen. ***What Was the Boston Tea Party?*** New York: Grosset & Dunlap, 2013.

*Yomtov, Nel. ***Plymouth Rock: What an Artifact Can Tell Us About the Story of the Pilgrims.*** Mankato, MN: Capstone Press, 2022.

Websites

Bunker Hill Monument: www.nps.gov/bost/learn/historyculture/bhm.htm

Faneuil Hall: www.nps.gov/bost/learn/historyculture/fh.htm

The Freedom Trail: www.thefreedomtrail.org

The Mayflower Society: themayflowersociety.org/about